SEEDS OF THE POMEGRANATE

SHERRY LAZARUS ROSS

Best wishes,
Sherry L. Ross

WELL FIRE PUBLICATIONS

Seeds of the Pomegranate

2nd Edition 2004
First Published 2000

ISBN=0-615-11133-5

Published by Well Fire Publications
100 Markley Street, Port Reading, N.J. 07064

Printed by BANTA BOOKS

For
My mother Marjorie
and
My daughter Kara

Acknowledgments:

I want to thank my husband Fred for being my steadfast supporter and best friend, my son Greg who is also a poet and who's attention to detail has been immensely constructive, to my dad Leon, writer and friend, and my sister Rochelle, also a writer and friend, for their support and love. I would like to acknowledge my appreciation to Martin S. Willick, who has continually urged me to finish this project, and also to my poetry workshop group for their companionship in the art of poetry, their constructive editorial help with several of these poems, and our continued work together. We are the Montclair Poetry Workshop, founded by Broeck Wahl Blumberg. The other members are Lauren A. Cerruto, Kathy Gilligan, Donna Larsen, Deborah Greenhut, and Megan Duffy. Also, love in memory of my cousin Annie Jenks for all the love she gave me.

S.L.R.

TABLE OF CONTENTS

FORWARD

The classical Greek myth of Persephone had a powerful impact on me as a child. My mother read to me most of the Greek myths as bedtime stories when I was four and five years old. These myths became a part of my internal world. The story of Persephone is filled with intrigue, passion, abduction, fierce love and revenge – all played out within the family triangle. No wonder its impact on me was strong.

Persephone was the daughter of Zeus, the most powerful of the gods, and Demeter, the Earth goddess. Zeus, without telling Demeter, promised their daughter to Hades, the god of the underworld and the dead, when she reached young womanhood. One afternoon, as the beautiful young Persephone picked flowers by the riverside, Hades rose out of the ground on his chariot and took her by force to his realm.

When Demeter learned of her daughter's disappearance she became grief stricken. She didn't know where to find her. Demeter searched the world for her beloved daughter. She was so filled with rage and grief that she neglected her duties as a goddess and the Earth became barren and infertile. All crops withered, animals could not have offspring, and death came after man.

Finally Demeter went to Zeus and he confessed to his secret contract with Hades. Demeter was furious and Zeus said she could travel to Hades and reclaim their daughter. Demeter made the trip to Hades, and crossed the River Styx that separated the living from the dead, on Charon's (the ferryman's) boat. The dead, in Greek mythology, had to pay Charon a gold coin for the trip or they would not be allowed to enter Hades.

When Demeter reached her daughter and confronted Hades, Hades did not want to give Persephone up. He loved her deeply. Persephone, who had been desolate and lonely, had hardly eaten. But with Hades prompting, she gave in and ate six seeds from the pomegranate fruit that grew in Hades. It was a law that if you ate the food of the dead you must remain with the dead. Even Zeus had to respect this law. But Hades took pity on Demeter and Persephone. This was his realm, and only he could strike a bargain. He said that for six months Persephone could return to the upper world with her mother, but for six months, one month for each seed, she must return to him. The women gladly accepted and Persephone agreed to return of her own free will.

Hence, the seasons were born. When summer ends, and Persephone returns to Hades, fall begins and passes into winter. But Demeter's grief is now not so great or destructive, because she knows in six months her daughter will return. When Persephone returns to Earth, Demeter rejoices and brings forth spring.

To me the story of Persephone is also a story of strength and healing. Persephone adapts. After all, she has become the great Queen of the Underworld and shares her power with her husband Hades, who grieves for her when she leaves to spend her time with Demeter. And when she returns to her mother, she is the catalyst for rebirth, fertility and joy.

S.L.R.

PERSEPHONE

Mother,
you've seen the sky in Hades.
Its inky abyss is reflected
on the River Styx. Through it
is a pathway to your world.

Yes,
there is great sorrow here.
First I sat bewildered on my
throne and lost all
sense of boundaries.

The endless crossings, the
mountains of useless coins
almost broke me.
But now I'm glad I
ate the blood red eggs.

This is as it should be.
I am the queen and must
listen to the silent
heartbeat of my realm.
Only I can hear it.

Mother,
you needn't grieve for me
while I'm away.
I've come to love my work.
Hades and myself are one.

There is beauty in this
underside - so much more
than sorrow. It is a world of
lost and found - the lost
stay lost until I find them.

I am the filter through which
all souls must pass. I
recognize their value,
raise my scepter,
split the sky.

Cobalt blue the
underworld rips open,
a path through which
I send my treasures
up to you.

Mother,
I am your one
true daughter.
I live in two worlds now,
they both are mine.

In late winter
I will bring you courage.
Be proud.

LIGHT & DARK

A child halts at the
edge of a forest, end of a field.
Sweat runs down her legs.
She ran so swiftly her abrupt
stop nearly toppled her into the
darkness.

She wonders why the dark
arose so rudely.
How does a wall of wood
replace a length of grass?
She doesn't know a field holds
boundaries of stop and go.

Her arms reach out for balance.
The grass is gone, but here
instead a drapery of leaves
appears, a party dress of
hunter green waiting to be worn.

Beyond her view water
makes its coy gurgle of
enticement. The curtain parts.
"Remember us?" rustle trees.
Light glitters on wet rocks.
Minnows twitch in the creek.
Tiger lilies splash orange.
"Come in, play hide-and-seek."

One step more, she takes it.
The trance of sunlight breaks,
brings forgetfulness of open fields,
distant voices, summer games.
She enters a palate of light & dark.

HEART OF SUMMER IN SAN GIMIAGNO

Marble table,
hypnotic swirls of
red and white,
Jupiter's surface.
Ripe fruit in a yellow bowl,
sticky plums, flies, a bit of mold.
Wine in a clay pitcher,
an ancient shape,
the potter's thump,
fragments of poetry.
Streets deserted,
hush, thick heat, it's lunch time, a
noon sun conquers,
defeats the weak,
bakes ambition,
slides down old walls,
trees, buildings with
dark windows and cracks the
color of bleached bone.
Shadows lay heavy,
the big meal,
blue dish with a crust of bread,
narcotic sleep,
arms and head against
cool marble, the
hum of sun,
light,
bees,
fruit flies,
Jupiter.

VIEW FROM THE BOARDWALK

When waves hit granite a
sound so sorrowful emerges
it feels like grief. A moan
rises then drops, woeful
vibration pulsing
downward under the
liquid shimmer of sea.

Children laugh and play
along the beach,
sand between their toes
still warm from the
day's heat.
They run, shout, a dog barks,
grains of joy.

Evening chills small
shoulders feverish and sun
burnt. Hungry they gather
plastic pails, shovels red
and green. They leave a
little older, their skin
smelling of salt,
sea decay.

It's show time now,
the sun's one act play of
drowning repeated every
night. The fire maiden
dissolves from red to
purple into Neptune's
dark wet chest.

Excitement ignites like
carnival rides or the smell of
seafood, meat and French fries
grilled and sizzling to completion.
There are games to play, a
prize for every bull's eye.
Empty peanut shells and beer
cans litter the ground, but who can
sleep while a bright Ferris wheel
turns in the dark?

Near morning when time
bends itself through lidded
windows, brief sleep will force us
to a place where some of what has
burdened us is thrown away in
dreams. Here we swim like eels,
electric impulses in our own debris.

Morning comes gold and sweet.
A man who owns a diner
is up early. He sweeps away peanut
shells that lie about his door. His
son sings something familiar, collects
beer cans and puts them in the bin
marked "Recycle." The perfect
smell of coffee pours out into the air
and down the boardwalk.

Sometimes life is simple,
coffee and a Danish, a
grain of joy melting
on the tongue.

GRAND FINALE

Stockholm August, 1994

How exquisite!
This wrought iron lamp with its
filigree finial
casts a delicate image on the
hotel room ceiling:
fishbone
snowflake
Nordic star,
symbols of summer
ending.

The Inlet Nörrstrom
is filled with
water festival
music,
twirling lights,
fireworks.

From the window an
image to remember:
my ten-year-old
daughter in her
pink nightgown and
acrylic jacket
running with her
dad into the
street crowd to
watch the
grand finale.

END OF SUMMER
Glen Devon, Scotland

Cool clouds fall,
moist dimensions built of
blue light, fog and
mystery. These are air
caves in a landscape of
temporality. Watch, they
sink into gold and brown
mounds of aged heather, then
merge with the earth of
ancient solid glen.

Small creatures
fall too into this
valley of earth flesh, the
shadow of clouds
move over them and change the
shape of what they are.
Seeds
pull themselves into the
tightening ground,
signals of
transition and descent.

DEATH AND HIS DIRECTOR

"I can't let go, but
how I want to. The
garden is overgrown with August."

("Leave! I'm done with you.")

"I must cut this tangle
down, but I stand motionless,
languid liquor of
thick, fruity air
leaves me lifeless."

("Exit. You are not wanted here.")

"My limbs are weighted.
I stare ahead
embalmed in stagnant air,
something rots beneath me,
I won't look where."

(Go! I command you.")

"Let it all end. This
green madness
sick with mold and
root decay. I hear the frenzied
mouths chew - listen - a billion
dying bugs."

("Why do you disregard my words?")

"It must end.
Give me a cool moment, a
breath of air not tainted with the
orchard's smell of over-ripeness. Let me
instead be alert with cold tomorrow."
("You haven't fooled me. I know you're there
behind the arbor.")

"All right.
All right. I'm ready.
Bring me my scythe.
Bring me my hood.
It's time to do what
I must do.
Soon the farmers will want to
celebrate their harvest."

("Finally!")

ENDINGS

Between the edge of the red leaf and the
start of the surrounding space
lies a fine line of shimmer, an unstable place
where you may pass through into the mystery.

Branches, half empty,
weave a tangle of black lace across
dusk, hold back that final
storm meant to sweep clean the last of autumn.

I take the front path and break the long
day's labor of a spider's intricate work. The
threads make me jump, tickle unpleasantly.
I wipe my face instinctively many times.

These signs say an era ends. The air's
breath is harsh and beautiful, strong and sharp.
Cold clouds contract, celestial density, clear design,
they move with purpose and resolve.

There can be great excitement in endings -
especially in that instant just before the end,
when mystery passes through your edges,
then moves on.

LEAF MADNESS

They're down,
all of them,
little curled seed wrappers,
little brown bug blankets
piling higher.
What a world this is:
landscape of pointed fingers,
squirrel castles.
The neighbor's dog
plunges in and
knows ecstasy,
crisp bits and
burrs
sticking to his fur.
Here is a madness to
indulge in;
it's natural for this world
to disengage and
fall apart.
Watch the treetops
stretch with freedom.
They're on vacation,
shake their arms with
clear amusement as
we rake and rake.

IN ONE DAY

In one day
I filled with grief, a
loss too primitive to define,
had my hair plaited into an
elaborate French braid,
imagined a lover I never had,
felt chilled, draped my old
plaid cape from Scotland around
my shoulders and fell asleep on the
couch in the middle of the day,
awoke, startled by an odd prickly tingle in
my fingers, ate two pretzels because they
had no fat, ate two chocolate covered
biscotti because they do have fat,
arranged dried flowers and seeds along the
fireplace mantle, laughed so hard at a stupid
joke that I had to run to the bathroom,
listened to a lot of people attentively,
ordered (not cooked) dinner,
sang,
told a lot of people I wasn't interested in
what they had to say, watched my husband and
daughter carve the pumpkin,
stuffed a gorilla
costume,
toasted
pumpkin seeds,
wrote this poem,
curled in my husband's
arms like a sleepy
squirrel.

THANKSGIVING

Twelve loaves of bread:
cranberry
apple walnut
pumpkin
banana
ginger-pear
oatmeal raisin -
two of each.

All the while I knead
I imagine your warm hands,
the way they comfort me.

I lay the harvest table:
lemons and pears adorn the
holly and bay leaf,
beautiful branches arranged
against white linen,
columns of lit candles
erect between the greens.

There is an exquisite feel to the
placement of silverware, the
surface of lemons, the
tiny shallow pits of their
pulpy skin, the
smoothness of pears by
contrast, the
prick of the holly leaf.

What richness we have.
Today the banquet of
family ritual,
tonight,
just us.

GRIEFS

I hold a perfect
acorn by its stem, a
plump green olive in a
wooden bowl.
I remember my mother
wearing acorn earrings and the
pewter tray filled with olives
green and black on
our Thanksgiving table.

This year there are signs
missing, old symbols lost:
collections of bright red leaves,
milkweed pods and brilliant
bittersweet. Where is the
nesting instinct to decorate with
gourds, dried herbs, willow branches,
pumpkins and pomegranates?

Waiting for the first snow
is painful in this new season.
No excitement in the silver winter
solstice, no holiday card
sent in ritual contract.
Persephone returns each spring -
her contract is eternal:

But I cannot
return to you.

PANDORA'S BOX

All that should be buried is,
the bulbs deep within their
nests of earth and
bone meal.

Pandora herself so small
what remains fits within the
golden box – just
dust and hair.

The mulch of leaves is under the
stiffened holly bush, the
burlap is around the dormant
rose tree.

Everything seems in its place.
From the corner of my eye
I see a silhouette move on the
horizon and feel a shiver.

SNOW QUEEN

The statues hold council in the
sculpture garden:
spring, summer, winter, fall,
they mark the circular pathway.

Winter now takes precedence,
her garments drape
weighted around her graceful
shoulders, smoke pot in her hands.

She reminds me of the Snow Queen
proud and keeping secrets.
She understands the intricate shape of
every snowflake ever made.

All leaves are swept away, the
garden is immaculate,
pristine, its architecture evident:
paths, gates, lamp-posts, pillars.

Listen! No leaf-blowers,
no town pick-up trucks
grinding in the distance, only a
pause before an entrance.

The air has changed over into
this ice new moment, the
animals, hushed, stay still
frozen with respect.

The sky is so white it is like
magic and heartache
contained in dreams of
pleasure marred with terror.

Now it begins, the
first falling crystal gifts of
danger, risk, a lifetime of
holiday fevers into the darkness.

Look closely at the Snow
Queen's eyes, carved of marble
they somehow shift and look
askance at spring.

WINTER ANGEL

Each hour the
waterfall
grows more solid,
liquid turned luminous ice.

Thickened sides
fold inward around the
moving force,
gigantic crystal wings.

Inside the frozen
center the water's
soul still
pours and sings.

Winter angel
waiting to release.

NIGHT FEAST
Midnight Hour

It is the hour of watchfulness.
Time is not as we know it in the day.
The eye opens in the dark.
It sees itself in all things moonlit.

Downstairs the front door opens.
The leopard slides into the center hall.
Her ears hear where warm hearts sleep.
She claims herself in all that is.

It is the beechnut tree who sent her.
Its roots can suck the truth from us,
then manifest it in the dark.
Its copper leaves conduct feeling.

Upstairs
blood pools in the cool bed.
Remember,
this is night feast.

INSOMNIA

There is only now:
moon with its lid of clouds,
pond with its midnight fish,
earth with its dead and dormant,
heart with its hurt.

PREPARATIONS

Around me
stands the architecture of my life:
this hundred year old house
holds memories unknown to me
yet I call it mine.
Paintings
place me in a hall of time,
furniture, antiques
stained and carved,
held others' intimacies,
secret letters,
objects needed,
discarded.

Look at the garden
bathed in translucent
light, nostalgic, a lost place
found again. I hear
children's voices,
sound of buzz saw.
I have done this,
lost this
over and over, this
living.

I look into a painting,
see the dead artist.
I touch a piece of
furniture,
feel the unknown carpenter.
I sit in my garden,
become the stranger.
Even my children
were mine for such a
brief moment.

Truly I possess
nothing,
not even my own sweet
body
changing;
she will leave
me too.

LOOKING BACK

All I remember is this:
moments of hurt,
moments of intimacy.
Where are the details of
daily life?

They fall away:
seeds from the pod,
leaves from the tree,
wheat from the stalk.
What then remains?

Elemental forms:
pod,
silhouette of trees, the
stalk. A
field of feelings.

Scavenger of detail,
I pick beneath the dried
remains and hunt its empty
shells and husks for memories:

Coffee cups the size of soup bowls, a
breakfast in Normandy, everything
blue and white.
My son,
ten months old,
frightened by hot
pink zinnias. An
elegant patio meal,
my daughter
tempting ducks with
French bread and brioche,
till she held one squawking on
her lap.

Hanging our first painting.
Ice over the waterfall.
The first kiss.
The last nursing.
The taste of basil.
The smell of lichen.

I cannot say I
know my life
exactly as it was,
but I can say I
know it well.

SUNDAY IN JANUARY

There are mouths
never to be tasted that
would suit us to perfection.
It is much the same
never to have
seen the Aurora Borealis or
great temples of the East.

Pick your place, your mouth.

Is this a loss?
So much undone?
It begins to snow –
snow in January
saddens the heart,
unlike December
snow which courts
adventure.

South of the equator –
switch what you
know of months.

The bear is lucky.
He sleeps till it is
wake up time or
doesn't wake at all.
We all wish death to
come like this.

The fireplace –
the fire.
Have we all dreamed of
love here?

I find one pine
needle stuck between two
cracked tiles in the hearth.
The mantle still holds
pine cones. The rest of
holiday is packed away.

Many plans have been
dismantled in a single life.
The fullest life can only
hold so much; so much or
it will come undone.

GHOST TALK

Two female ghosts
sit on my closed-in porch,
crossed legs
short skirts
very stylish.
They discuss me as if
I'm not here.

They speak with a critic's
voice, discerning,
dissecting, just the right
inflection of
exasperation.
Their neat-to-the-chin
haircuts swivel in
unison from side to side,
displaying disapproval.

I am a flaky
find, a new
restaurant-worth-trying, but
they doubt I'll survive.
I have my strong points,
not-worth-three-stars,
bring-your-own-wine,
good-appetizer
too-much-sauce-on-the-entrée
type of place with
middle range
ambiance.

I am furious!

"Where do you come off,
here in my own home,
scaring the wits
out of me for days,
finally,
you make yourselves
known and you have nothing
better to say than this?
Well, I'll just ask you to
leave, thank you."

They keep on talking:
"Too kitschie
for my taste,
but sometimes she's
endearing."
"Too cluttered to be
truly tasteful."
"Her sense of color
is well defined but
she always goes one
step too far!"
"Doesn't know
when to quit,
does she?"

"Get out!"
I scream on the
top of my lungs.

They turn briefly
startled,
mostly bored.

"Where did you come from?"
I demand.

They look straight through
me and speak in turns.
"You know that edition
you just had to have, dear?"
"The big room with just a
few too many details, Luv?"
"Well, when they dug it up
they dug us up."
"Here we are!"
"But don't mind us."
"Just get on with
your life."
"Please,
we're waiting."

OUT AND OUT

Pepper cloud of birds,
who shakes you out
across this sky?
Thick clouds
sweet and rich
I put my
mouth to you,
drink you like a milkshake.
White sun,
winter sun,
my life is flowing
out and out,
fills in again from
somewhere,
I fling myself at
you and burn and
burn.

FEBRUARY'S FUTURE

Light is steel blue in the
soon to snow sky,
tracks of branches
crisscross, make contacts
connections that carry an
urge for adventure.

Galaxies disperse energy
out of elliptical forces.
My ovaries release
eggs with great speed,
accelerated cycles of
last chances.

Lightning jump-started
Earth's atmosphere:
old-fashioned evolution.
Soon we'll burn CD's of
snowflakes, each sound
unique as it falls.

RETURN TRIP

The road is crammed with traffic.
On either side smokestacks hurl
ever changing sculpture into the
cold air. Factories' massive pipes
grow dark as charcoal sketches.
The day slides down, covers ugly
sights with a soft wash of purple
shadow. Birds descend on garbage
heaps - small gods on small mountains.
Trees stroke the sky with branch
tips. The sun tares from out a
bank of swollen clouds, a sudden
birth red, wet, and round.

MARCH

Trees
defrost
tangle into each other
ignite
know some non-verbal
push to wake.
A pigeon calls its mate
across the neighbor's roof.
Queen bee still sleeps
her dreams swelling.
Buds make their slow
move to split open.
There is death even now.
The sun does its work.
So does the ground.

TOUCH ME

How many times can the earth
withstand this ritual? The
pain of being frozen, then
thawed out.

The trowel
up-turns the first
signs of life, old
bits of death.

Listen! The
ground stirs, the
trowel works.

Here is dead wood to
cut away – brittle or
soft with rot.

Smell of dirt,
smell of minerals –
so clean!
Not as we've been taught.

Run your fingers
through the dark grains,
comb it through.
Tend to it.

Here – a discovery,
tuber roots.
What plant is this?
It will know.

There is so much
dependability in this
vast expanse of land.
Unexpected blooms as well.

Do you hear the
wake up call?
It's as soft as the
turn of earthworms.

There is a pull from
sleep to waking as
death falls and
life lifts up.

"touch me,"
calls the thawing ground.
"I'm so tender."

ENTRANCE

Infant leaves
bleed into a shimmering sky.
Black pond is
deeper than a coal mine.

The oak breaths.
Its see-through frills
contract, expand with
green longing.

There is hunger in this
turn of seasons as the
earth splits with
pain, delivery.

There is hunger in this
slow motion of the
earth aching to
begin again.

Pulsing sun,
Celestial heart,
pumps life into
all matter.

SPRING

Outside
branches spread and
suck light,
nursing on the sun.
Inside
myself
I feel the ping of a
ripe ova.
I imagine the
little wound on
my ovary.

TAPESTRY

All my childhood
I longed to be the
Holy Hermit in the
lonely wood
seeing few but those
who sought me for
enlightenment.

But I was loved and
touched by hands
giving and taking
so that a weaving
intricate,
permanent,
wove me other than
I planned:

Wove me human,
touched, and
so imperfect.

FETAL MOVEMENT

She slips into the orange
light slumber of sealed
afternoon eyelids, feels the
baby thud gently against its
red onion skin home.

Sleep clasps its foam
rubber hands around
her and they fit perfectly,
soft upholstery around a
drum shaped hassock.

The fabric holds her still,
solid like sturdy furniture.
She rests while they both
change, growing clearly
more and more apart.

CREEPING THYME

I plant you on the
hill and find
you on the patio
four years later,
pushed up between
slate cracks.

You spread out,
toward, and away,
soft and wild
especially after
spring rain. A
fragrant throw.

My daughter
has this knowledge.
She is soft and wild,
grows double wise and
shows herself in
unexpected places.

MAYPOLE

Field of bayonets,
hard green tips
erect, aroused, piercing
out of the wet ground.
This is a surprise of
pantomime , tomorrow
they will be dressed in
drag, daffodil skirts
ruffled, waving and coy.
Nature flirts from every
point, with whom to what,
what matters? All is
primp and posturing,
parade of show-and-tell.

This is the ancient May pole
dance, outrageous, blunt, intent.
This is that joyous part of spring
when all is innocent.

SPRING CACTUS

Desert plant,
young root herb,
your hollow fingers
dig into the sand,
clutch, barely hold
you up. Your
tongue has learned to
drink sand, to
taste the countless
edges of a million
grains of rock that
burn, but never fill
you up. Yet your
flesh grows full, your
brilliant blooms of
heat appear across your
breast, and draw the
admiration of the
passing
cactus
wren.

WHOOSH AND GONE

Here I go
arms stretched
wide over the furrowed
earth damp with last
night's rain and the
juice of broken insects.
Sweep,
sweep,
out,
this sky
is a sky of
boundlessness,
a sky of
whoosh and gone.
Right now I
skim the ground
my belly
close to the
turned dirt I love.
My fingers
pump air.
Below me
people work,
their backs bent
they hoe and rake,
scrape and break
insect parts
unknowingly.
Out of torn
ground
jut bulbs of
bones,
heads of
pipes,
nails.

Last year's
dried leaves
fly at me and hit
harmlessly like
empty paper bags.

Larvae make their
bodies twist up and
free.
Twigs,
pebbles,
lost feathers
scatter under
me as
I gain
speed,
break
out into the
green
light of a
green
field, with
nothing
ahead
but
unobstructed
air.

PRIMITIVE

This is how it is to
put your tongue in the
blood of feelings:
the spider in her web,
the sparrow in her nest,
the fish beneath the ice,
the words between
your heart and mouth before
they're spoken.

This is how it is to
put your tongue in the
blood of feelings:
the spider waits,
the sparrow waits,
the fish wait, but
eventually the
spell is broken.

This is how it is to
put your tongue in the
blood of feelings:
the spider feeds,
the sparrow leaves,
the fish spawn, so
speak the words
that must be spoken.

MYTH

Always the rainbow
brings with it a legend.
Here in this land of
fractured light and moisture
rainbows happen all the time.
Still, we stop and point and say,
"Look, a rainbow!" and a
myth in us rises.

IN GALLOWAY FOREST, SCOTLAND

Crouched,
I see the wood is old:
old and everywhere.

First observe the hushed nest of
one-hundred years of pine needles.
They have fallen season after season as
petals falls, caught on felled branches,
piled higher each year,
mounds and mounds of needles
how many feet deep by now?
I balance on a web of branches,
boots buried in a sunken arc
burdened with my human weight.
This feels precarious.
One false move and I might
slip under and become
lost in the roots forever.

Look.
The light now is
pink and silver.
It is everywhere.

The light has turned
silver/gold and the
needles glow pink like
sunset. The world is
leaving me, darkening.
I feel this wood is haunted.

The light calls me to follow.
Is this my father or my mother?
I am the lost child of all stories.
The light is so beautiful it has
become a sound.

Music.
Listen.
It is a deep sound first, of
roots,
trees, then the
ecstasy of sky.

The sound enters me and
fills me up like a hundred
years of pine needles till
I am so full I become
pink, gold, silver and light.
I am not haunted, but
returned. Returned with
so much to discover,
so much to grieve,
everywhere.

NECTAR AND ASH

You are the holy
ghost of your own
being.
You hover inside
yourself -
hummingbird within
nectar.

You fill yourself with
juice and ash,
fecund
composite of
layered
living.

Watch the moss that
grows in mounds:
ferns unfold,
wings hover.
Hear the sound of
swift blood -
trees filled with
animation.

Everything moves,
is filled with
nectar and ash.
It is on us.
It is now.

DEMETER

I miss the soft mornings we
sat near the Gulf of Volos.
I brushed your thick auburn
hair down to your waist.
It curled so sweetly at the tips.
I can still smell the lovely warm
smell of your little girl scalp.

You wove reed jewelry for me,
remember?
Bracelets, bracelets and rings.
You said I never had enough.
Sometimes you would tuck
flowers into the braids at my
wrist and call them sapphires,
rubies, emeralds.

Daughter,
The terror I felt
when you were taken from me
made evil reach inside my chest and
steal my heart. I wandered empty,
dazed, then emptiness turned to rage.
What was it I forgot to do
that let this happen?

Anger,
I turned it all on
what was mine.
My world suffered greatly
that first time.